THE GROWING CONGREGATION

THE GROWING CONGREGATION

PAUL BENJAMIN

LINCOLN CHRISTIAN COLLEGE PRESS
Lincoln, III.

DEDICATED

With deep affection

to my father-in-law

O. S. Lincoln

FOREWORD

"The church must grow!" is the impassioned plea of the author, Paul Benjamin.

Dr. Benjamin was born in the parsonage. His parents placed within his heart a concern for the lost and a great love for the Church of Jesus Christ. It has been my privilege to know this man since boyhood. I have seen his passion for evangelism grow from a little flame to a tremendous fire.

Some may look askance at this book because it seems revolutionary. Others will realize that in order to spread the gospel of Christ around the world in our time, the congregation must first be galvanized into action.

Today, many Christians are feeling the urgency to reach out to others. Dr. Benjamin has shown us the principles which will allow us to break the traditions which bind us and launch us into a dynamic movement which can yet carry out our Lord's desire for global evangelism.

The book is logical, scriptural, and practical. God's people should read and study its contents prayerfully.

Dr. Earl C. Hargrove, Chancellor
Lincoln Christian College
Lincoln Christian Seminary

PREFACE

This study of some basic principles of church growth is related primarily to the activity of the American church. Such a viewpoint is in no way intended to negate the global commission of Jesus Christ. Rather, I have chosen North America simply as one starting point for fulfilling his Great Commission.

Very little doubt exists in my mind but that the American church is a sleeping giant. Stirred into action, it could produce in our times the most sweeping spiritual, social, economic, and political changes in the history of the world. This world is waiting for such a revolution. Jesus used ordinary men for extraordinary tasks from the very beginning, and he also is waiting for his followers today to do the extraordinary.

This book has been planned for varied use. It can be read by individuals simply as a book, or it can serve as a guide to discussion for a group. Congregations are looking today for study materials on church growth. This study may be used by them on Sunday morning in an adult or older youth class which follows a thirteen week quarter. Teacher and students can follow a chapter each week and use the corresponding discussion section as the lesson for the following week. Most Sunday School classes are long on lecture and short on discussion. This book is designed to help remedy that problem. Some congregations may find this study useful in their mid-week service or home Bible study gatherings.

It will be tragic if the use of the study makes no difference in the **action** of the average congregation. This study has not been designed as merely an exercise in thinking; it has been designed to help congregations relate their own congregational life to Christ's imperative of seeking and winning the lost.

Certain presuppositions held by the author are nowhere stated in the text. I am presupposing that readers believe in God, in his only begotten son Jesus Christ, and in the person and power of the Holy Spirit. I am also presupposing that the people who read and discuss these pages have a concern for the lost. Nothing can stimulate a congregation into action which perpetually operates at a low level of concern.

The terminology ''church growth'' is rapidly becoming a catch-all phrase in some circles to indicate **all** the activity carried on by the church. I feel that such expansiveness is unwarranted and deprives this phrase of its cutting edge—the discipling of the lost for Christ. It is in this latter and narrower sense that I have sought to employ this expression for my study.

Readers who desire more technical information than may be found in the text of this study are encouraged to turn to the section of footnotes and references. Reading suggestions, as well as references to more detailed discussion elsewhere, are available there.

ACKNOWLEDGEMENTS

I am deeply indebted to many people who have assisted in the preparation and printing of this book. Earl Hargrove was the first to read the manuscript for content. John Ralls has made many valuable suggestions for style. Enos Dowling has called my attention to source material in evangelism. Charliene Donaldson typed the manuscript, Joe and Maxine Seggelke were responsible for printing, and Julian Gee did the art work.

Numerous congregations and hundreds of pulpit ministers in America have heard me expound these ideas. I have gained much through sharing sessions.

My wife Lois and I started walking four or five miles daily several years ago; on these walks, in all kinds of Illinois weather, she has served as a testing ground for my ideas on church growth.

I am also grateful to Charlie Shedd, Elton Trueblood and Floyd Thatcher. These veterans gave me encouragement in writing at a time when I needed it most.

November 15, 1971

CONTENTS

I

CHURCH GROWTH
AND THE NEW TESTAMENT CONGREGATIONS

Beginnings

Any discussion of the growing congregation must take into account that unique Biblical book entitled THE ACTS OF THE APOSTLES. The conduct of the disciples at the death of Jesus Christ makes even the reality of such a book most surprising.

The gospel writers describe the sorry behavior of the disciples while Jesus suffers alone. They all fall asleep during his agony in the Garden of Gethsemane. They scatter like frightened sheep during his trial. Peter denies him with a curse. Afraid of the bitter wrath of the Jewish leaders, they cower behind closed doors (John 20:19). A few days later, this same group of intimidated men are boldly proclaiming salvation through Jesus of Nazareth in the streets of Jerusalem.

What can possibly account for such a remarkable change in attitude? We can turn to purely naturalistic explanations in vain. The broken hopes of all the faithful are summarized in the expression of those two followers who had left Jerusalem for Emmaus on the Sunday following the crucifixion: "But we had hoped that he was the one to redeem Israel" (Luke 24:21). Only a miracle could revive such despair—a miracle which in actuality had already happened, although they did not realize it. The miracle of miracles happened when God raised Jesus bodily from the grave (Acts 2:24).

The reality of the resurrection was impressed upon the disciples in different ways and at different times. Once, on the shores of Lake Galilee, Jesus ate breakfast with his disciples following his resurrection (John 21:9f). Writing to the Christians in Corinth, Paul mentions some of the appearances of Jesus after his resurrection: "he appeared to Cephas, then to the twelve. Then he appeared to more than five hundred brethren at one time, most of whom are still alive, though some have fallen asleep. Then he appeared to James, then to all the apostles. Last of all, as one untimely born, he appeared also to me" (I Cor. 15:5-8).

No wonder the disciples had something to tell others. They had seen Christ alive again in the flesh after his death, just as he had promised! More than that, his resurrection gave the basis for the realization that all his other promises must be

2

true. So, they not only preached; they could not stop preaching (Acts 4:20).

After his resurrection, Jesus gave his disciples global evangelizing commissions. In Galilee, he instructed his followers to "make disciples of all nations" through teaching and baptizing and teaching (Matt. 28:19). Back in Judea, just prior to his ascension, Jesus told his disciples to be his witnesses "in Jerusalem and in all Judea and Samaria and to the end of the earth" (Acts 1:8).

The Phenomenal Expansion of the Gospel

The geographical compass of the New Testament congregations is a phenomenon of its own. A few years after Jesus gave his global evangelizing commissions in Palestine, Paul is writing to Christians in Rome (Rom. 1:7). That the gospel has gone as far as Rome in such a short time demonstrates the type of evangelistic zeal which these early Christians possessed. In spite of the barrier of distance in apostolic times (it took about five days to walk from Nazareth to Jerusalem, a distance of 75 miles), by the end of the first century, the Mediterranean had become a "Christian" lake.

ACTS records Jesus' parables of salt and light exploded into action. The growth from the 120 in the upper room through the 3000 on the day of Pentecost to 5000 in Jerusalem then to Rome and

3

on to the end of the civilized world—in two generations—is a story which bears retelling. Many of these accomplishments were made during times of persecution. Christianity became an illegal religion before the first century was over. Many faced death for their faith. In spite of a culture which was often hostile, the gospel continued to penetrate society.

Some of the finest testimonies to the missionary courage of the early disciples come from their enemies. After being commanded by the Sanhedrin "to speak no more to any one in this name" (Acts 4:17), the apostles are later hailed into court with the charge, "you have filled Jerusalem with your teaching" (Acts 5:28). In Thessalonica, the opponents to Paul and his helpers report the rumor which was circulating widely throughout the city, "These men who have turned the world upside down have come here also" (Acts 17:6).

The enemies of the cross made the situation for the spreading of the gospel very difficult at times. Paul can see, however, that sometimes even personal adversity can be used to help preach the gospel. A case in point is his visit to Rome. Wishing eagerly to preach the gospel in that queen of ancient cities, Paul saw his hopes utterly dashed when he becomes a political prisoner in Caesarea because of Jewish plots against him. Finally, his coveted desire to be in Rome becomes possible, but he arrives there, not as a a free man, but as a prisoner in chains. After his arrival, though, he saw the hand of God in guiding his destiny. As a bound prisoner in Rome, he wrote to his beloved Philippians, "I want you to know brethren, that what has happened to me has really served to advance the gospel" (Phil. 1:12). The renowned praetorian guard, the noblest and bravest among Roman soldiers, were hearing the gospel through Paul's imprisonment. And even more startling, converts were being made in Caesar's very household (Phil. 4:22).

The Vital Role of the Congregation

It is generally agreed among church historians that the New Testament period was one of the times of greatest expansion for the gospel. What is often overlooked during this period of tremendous growth is the vital part played by the congregation in helping to increase the number of believers.

The missionary journeys of Paul serve as an apt illustration of the importance of the congrega-tion. Paul's usual practice in bringing the gospel to a new territory was to preach first in the Jewish synagogue (Acts 17:2). He continued here until he was driven out, usually by the Jewish leaders who were envious of his influence (Acts 13:45; 17:5). Then Paul and those who believed his message began to meet elsewhere (Acts 17:7). A congregation was born which was often destined to have influence throughout an entire region (I Thess. 1:8).

Today, we sometimes see an emphasis which goes to an opposite extreme from Paul's concern for the congregation. Various kinds of programs of social concern are instituted by religiously minded people in order to serve a community. Many of these efforts are not designed to produce congregations of Christians. In fact, getting people as church members is sometimes looked upon as a prostitution of the gospel. In an area with few thriving congregations, such a procedure may be spiritually tragic.

It would be well at this point to remember Paul's practice. Were there no poor in the seaport city of Corinth? Were there no race problems in Ephesus? Did all the children in Asia Minor have enough to wear? Paul's letters to the congregations in various cities demonstrate his deep concern for the poor and socially disenfranchised (Gal. 2:10). He exhorts the Christians in Corinth to follow the example of other congregations in taking up a generous offering for the poverty-stricken saints in Jerusalem (II Cor. 8 & 9). Yet, his uniform practice in spreading the gospel of love and brotherly concern was to establish congregations. To ignore the apostolic practice, then, is to overlook the very heart of the methodology whereby the gospel spread around the Mediterranean in the first century. Furthermore, it overlooks a vital way by which the spiritual **and** physical needs of people may be met.

The Peril of Idealizing the Early Congregations

With all that may be said about the missionary zeal recorded in the New Testament, it is hazardous to idealize the first century church. The writers of the New Testament clearly indicate that the early congregations faced many serious problems. Lying (Acts 5:1f), racism (Acts 11:19), uninformed leaders (Acts 19:1f) are a part of the early Christian church.

Paul's first letter to Corinth reveals a startling list of imperfections: division (1:10f), exalting human wisdom (1:18f), spiritual immaturity (3:1f), immorality (5:1f), lawsuits between brothers (6:1f), faulty concepts of marriage (7:1f), problems regarding food offered to idols (8:1f), complaints about paying ministers (9:1f), drunkenness at the Lord's Supper (11:1f), jealousy over spiritual gifts (12:1f), disruption about tongues (14:1f), and false teaching about the resurrection of Christians (15:1f).

To hold the New Testament as our guide in church growth certainly would not include the continuation of many of the practices by the Corinthian congregation. Rather, it is the apostolic directives in dealing with these abuses which helps give direction to congregations today.

The Role of the Congregation Today

God's methodology in redeeming a lost society is still bound up in the role of the congregation. That role must include bringing men to God through "the obedience of faith" in Jesus Christ (Rom. 16:26). The Holy Spirit calls upon the congregation in Antioch to "Set apart for me Barnabas and Saul for the work to which I have called them" (Acts 13:3). Barnabas and Saul proclaim the word of God in the various cities and establish congregations of Christians as they travel. Thus, one congregation of Christians, by the sending out of its members, becomes directly responsible for the planting of many additional congregations.

No congregation can be unconcerned about the quality of its own congregational life. It is interesting to note that although individuals are sometimes mentioned, the seven congregations of Asia are graded as congregations. Philadelphia has been faithful to Christ's word (Rev. 3:8). Laodicea made the Lord sick (Rev. 3:16). The upgrading of congregational life is a continuing process demanding dedicated and forward looking leadership (I Tim. 3) and a willingness on the part of Christians to go on to maturity (Heb. 6:1f).

One of the great mysteries of the gospel is that God uses immature and imperfect people to bring others to the perfect Christ. If every congregation must retard its evangelistic endeavor until each member is perfect, then the Day of Judgment will arrive first. We sometimes forget that congregations are groups of forgiven sinners. Paul never forgot what he was before Christ changed his life (I Tim. 1:15-16). Our testimony to the outsider is not a recitation of our own goodness, but rather, a recital of the great saving acts of God through Christ whereby salvation is available to all (I Cor. 15:1-2). We continue in daily fellowship with God because of his daily forgiveness (Matt. 6:12).

An evangelistic outreach by the congregation which stresses a comfortable house of worship, a paved parking lot, an outstanding pulpit minister, an attractive youth program (or some similar emphasis) is to be faulted if the underlying spiritual purpose of the congregation is overlooked. A congregation serves as a lighthouse in pointing men to spiritual safety through Christ (I Tim. 1:15). A congregation which keeps pointing to itself misses the reason for its existence.

The New Testament and Church Growth

It goes without saying that the best book ever written on evangelism is the New Testament itself. To begin here is to start at the constitutional level.

No serious investigation of church growth can overlook the New Testament as the basic source-book. The New Testament must not be judged by any evangelistic emphasis being stressed today; rather, every evangelistic emphasis being stressed today must be continually judged by the New Testament.

Throughout the New Testament, certain basic principles of church growth relating to congregational life may be discovered. Having already reflected upon the phenomenal expansion of the church during the apostolic period, it will surely repay us to give close attention to these principles.

Often the principles for church growth in the New Testament impinge upon existing congregational practices which have been hallowed by long tradition. The crucial test which often presents itself to the leaders of a congregation is whether or not they are willing to revise their own practices in the light of New Testament teaching.

It is not customary for congregations to think about the source of many of their practices. Hence, any thinking at the source-level which would result in a change of procedure may be strenuously resisted. It has frequently been said that "heresy" may be a perfectly good doctrine overlooked for a generation.

Sad indeed is that congregation which thinks it has "arrived" in practicing New Testament doctrine. Such an attitude often leads to a spirit of complacency and sometimes downright Pharisaism which makes it exceedingly difficult for the Holy Spirit to work in congregational life. Continued willingness to learn from Christ (Eph. 4:20) keeps a congregation fresh and spiritually alert.

I am certainly not of the opinion that these are the **only** basic principles of church growth. Rather, I have chosen those concepts which are so frequently overlooked by the average congregation. It is my strong conviction that these ideas, once they are operative, can help to produce new life in the congregation and an outreach to thousands yet unreached.

THE PRINCIPLE OF GATHERING AND SCATTERING

The Method of Jesus

The procedure which Jesus followed in evangelizing is frequently overlooked today. He called two pairs of fishermen and promised to make them "fishers of men" if they would follow him (Matt. 4:18-22). After a night in prayer, he hand-picked twelve men from among his disciples to be "apostles (Luke 6:12-13). The verbal form of this word is significant. It means literally to "send away" or "send out." The intended purpose for the twelve is obvious from their collective name. They were to be sent out with the good news of the kingdom.

Jesus began by instructing the apostles. They followed him in his preaching journeys throughout Palestine and learned by listening and observing. He spent time with them in private (John 1:39). Later they received "on the field training" by being sent out into the towns and villages on missions of preaching and healing (Matt. 10:1f). Jesus followed a pattern of gathering and scattering. He gathered the apostles for prayer and instruction and scattered them in missions of service and preaching.

Later, in addition to the twelve, Jesus called. seventy others (Luke 10:1). An increase in his evangelistic outreach demanded an increase in the number of workers. Again, he followed the practice already established with the apostles. He sent the seventy out, two by two, into all the towns and villages with a message about the kingdom (Luke 10:9). Jesus, himself, would later visit those villages (Luke 10:1).

When Jesus chose the seventy, he repeated his concern for workers in the harvest given earlier to the twelve: "The harvest is plentiful, but the laborers are few; pray therefore the Lord of the harvest to send out laborers into his harvest" (Luke 10:2). It was when the seventy returned with a favorable report on their mission that Jesus predicted the ultimate fall of Satan by saying, "I saw Satan fall like lightning from heaven" (Luke 10:17).

The gospel writers are fairly explicit regarding the principle which Jesus followed in bringing the good news of the kingdom to others. He gathered men and instructed them. Then they were scattered to teach others. They returned for more instruction as a group and then went out to work again.

13

The Method of the Early Congregations

We have already referred to the method of Jesus in his "gathering-scattering" pattern. A similar method may be observed in ACTS. Luke says the early Christians "devoted themselves to the apostle's teaching and fellowship, to the breaking of bread and the prayers" (Acts 2:42). Paul preached in Troas until midnight to the disciples who had "gathered together to break bread" (Acts 20:7).

Here in the earliest history of the Christian church we find the pattern of gathering for worship which has helped characterize Christianity for nearly twenty centuries. Christians have always been a "gathering people," finding comfort and strength in God and in one another as they meet for thanksgiving, adoration, instruction, and inspiration.

We also find the early congregations were a "scattering church." The early Christians were continually spreading the good news of the gospel in the temple, in their homes, and in the streets (Acts 5:28;42).

When persecution drove the followers of Christ out of Jerusalem, Luke reports, "Those who were scattered went about preaching the word" (Acts 8:4). It is important to note that the antecedent of "those" is not the apostles. After a frightening experience with Peter and the other apostles, the rulers decided to leave them alone for a while. It was just ordinary Christians who went everywhere telling the good news of Jesus.

In all probability, the great missionary congregation in Antioch of Syria was planted by unknown Christians from ordinary walks of life. At first, the Christians who left Jerusalem preached only to Jews (Acts 11:19). Others, however, began preaching also to the Greeks (Acts 11:20). In Antioch where this combination resulted in great numbers turning to the Lord, Barnabas and Saul were later called to minister with a congregation **already established!**

Congregational Method Today

Comparatively speaking, few congregations today are following the New Testament principle of gathering and scattering. A study of congregational life in most religious groups usually reveals a "come-type" attitude. The faithful are exhorted weekly through the sermon, in the worship folder, and by the church paper to be "faithful to services." Much emphasis is placed upon "keeping up the attendance." A high attendance in proportion to the average is cause for elation, whereas a low attendance is cause for sagging spirits.

The "come-to-church" emphasis may be pictured as follows:

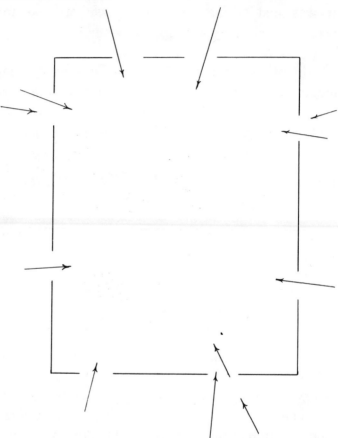

Note that all the arrows are "coming-in." "Come to the worship service, come to the mid-week service, come to the special preaching mission, come to the board meeting, come to the church fellowship, come, come, come!" The problem with the usual "come-type" emphasis is that attending the special functions of the congregation often becomes an end within itself.

In America, among numerous congregations, the "come-to-church" emphasis often results in stress laid upon three weekly services and giving a tithe of one's net income. I have often referred to this system as the "three and ten" pattern. The main difficulty with the "three and ten" pattern is the limits which it places upon participation in the kingdom of God. Furthermore, it often stresses one's relationship to the congregation rather than a personal relationship to Christ. A man may rise to a position of leadership in a congregation, even with very poor attitudes, if he attends the right number of services, and gives his money.

Pulpit ministers in American congregations who have helped devise and perpetuate the "come-to-church" emphasis are perhaps the ones who have suffered from it the most. The number of people present at stated services and the amount of the offering furnish the measuring rod whereby a congregation and the minister are judged a "success." These figures become the "spiritual statistics" of the congregation.

17

As long as the "spiritual statistics" are on the upswing, a minister feels secure with the congregation. But, alas, when the system fails him, he then feels he must look for a place of service elsewhere. An increasing number of American pulpit ministers are dejected today because they judge themselves failures according to their own standards of success. Preaching ministers sometimes forget that nowhere in the New Testament is the success of a Christian enterprise judged solely on the basis of the number of people meeting in one place.

Restoring the Method of Gathering and Scattering

An increasing number of congregations today are placing new stress upon individuals scattering as witnesses for Jesus Christ. Much like the early church which gathered for worship and scattered to witness, so increased emphasis is placed upon Christians bearing the good news of the gospel to others. The "come-to-church" emphasis is being balanced by a "go-in-witness" thrust. This emphasis may be pictured as follows:

THE PRINCIPLE OF GATHERING AND SCATTERING

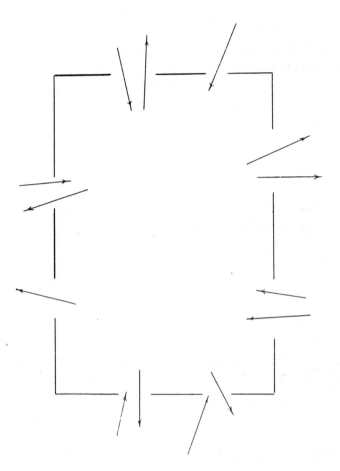

Note that the arrows are not only going in but they
are also going out. "Enter to worship, depart to
serve" has become a cliché, not an actual statement of congregational practice. Only when the
congregation begins to bear the good news of
Christ to the community can it truly be a Christian
congregation.

19

A congregation which moves to a method of worship and witness is taking nothing away from a pattern of worship. In fact, the worship services of a congregation increase in meaning as new people begin coming to Christ. As members see themselves doing the work of Christ in the community, a sense of purpose pervades the entire life of the congregation.

In working around the ''too-busy-to-evangelize'' syndrome which characterizes so many churches, a number of congregations have converted former worship-type services into witnessing services. Without minimizing the importance of every Christian bearing testimony for Christ in his daily routine, members of the congregation realize that thousands will never be contacted for Christ unless a systematic house-to-house plan is followed. Many congregations are transforming Wednesday and sometimes Sunday nights from a worship-type to a witnessing-type service. A block-plan is inaugurated in which teams of callers are sent out to gather information on each home in a particular block. They are also to bear a testimony for Christ. Additional teaching teams visit in the homes of the unchurched where people are responsive. It is very possible that a combination worship-witnessing type of service may be best of all. At the same time that some members of the congregation are in worship or study, others are out calling and witnessing.

Something very important usually happens in the life of the worshipper turned witness. He must examine his own faith to find whether or not he really has something vital to communicate regarding Christ. Often an intensified devotional life develops among those who realize the Lord is using them to minister to others. Religious discussion causes a witness to search the Scriptures daily as he becomes "a workman who has no need to be ashamed, rightly handling the word of truth" (II Tim. 2:15).

The Evangelistic Meeting

One of the instruments of God in bringing the gospel to millions on the North American continent is the evangelistic meeting. Great camp meetings characterized earlier generations of pioneers on the American frontier. Carried over into the twentieth century, these meetings became the "harvest-time" in thousands of communities. Yet, some very marked contrasts between the American evangelistic meeting and New Testament principles of church growth became apparent. These may be shown as follows:

Traditional Evangelistic Campaign	Campaigns Following Church Growth Principles
Emphasizes role of evangelist and his team	Emphasizes role of every Christian in witness
A few believers are motivated and sent out primarily to talk about the local church	All believers are motivated and sent out to talk primarily about Christ

Traditional Evangelistic Campaign	Campaigns Following Church Growth Principles
Broadens the audience of the gifted evangelist; multiplies his hearers	Multiplies the number of active evangelists; every hearer a proclaimer
Beguiles Christians into believing that they can pay others to carry out the Great Commission	Awakens Christians to the fact that no believer is exempt from carrying out the Great Commission
Tends to make evangelism seasonal; stops when the "campaign" is over	Emphasizes evangelism as a constant privilege and responsibility
Is not designed to mobilize the entire congregation in witness	Designed to mobilize the entire congregation in witness
Emphasizes gathering rather than scattering	Emphasizes gathering and scattering

Nothing should be done to minimize any method of evangelism which is bringing people to Christ. Many congregations, however, are at a loss in evangelism when they find the evangelistic meeting is no longer reaching the outsider for Christ. They sometimes wrongly conclude that evangelism itself is dead, when the problem in reality is related to a particular methodology.

Many congregations schedule extended services through the week, but their purpose varies from the traditional meeting. Instead of emphasizing "first principles," the dominant note is "going on to perfection." The fare for the congregational diet is meat, not milk (I Cor. 3:1). The saints are better equipped to minister (Eph. 4:11-12).

The congregational evangelistic meeting in some areas is a vital tool in reaching outsiders for Christ. Care must be exercised, however, lest the meeting becomes a substitute for house-to-house witnessing through the ministry of believers. Meanwhile, many congregations are re-examining their methodology in reaching others for Christ.   They are rediscovering the key to twentieth century evangelism in the New Testament.

III

THE PRINCIPLE OF THE MINISTRY OF ALL BELIEVERS

Examining the New Testament

One of the most encouraging developments taking place among many Christians today is a re-examination of the role of the ministry in the New Testament. Again and again across the centuries, the New Testament concept of the ministry of believers has been obscured. Nowhere in the Christian Scriptures do we find the kind of clergy-laity distinctions which are so familiar today.

The New Testament rings out with the idea of a serving people of God, not the creation of first and second class citizens in the kingdom of God. The prophet Joel looked forward to that time when God would pour out his spirit "on all flesh," including sons and daughters, old men and young men, and even servants (Joel 2:28-29). On the day of Pentecost, Peter announces that this revolutionary concept is now in operation (Acts 2:17-18).

The death knell to a special system of priests with a favored position before God was symbolized when Jesus hung on the cross and the great curtain in the temple which separated the holy place from the holy of holies was ripped in two (Luke 23:45). In the new dispensation, all of God's people are to be "a royal priesthood" (I Peter 2:9) with Jesus Christ functioning as the new high priest (Heb. 4:14).

It would be wrong, however, to assume that God's people are to function without leadership. Paul mentions James, Peter, and John with their reputation of being "pillars" in the church in Jerusalem (Gal. 2:9). The church at Antioch of Syria evidently had five strong leaders which included Barnabas and Saul of Tarsus (Acts 13:1). Apostles and prophets were part of the foundation of the church during the apostolic era (Eph. 2:20). These servants in the body of Christ, together with the evangelists and pastor-teachers, are regarded as Christ's "gifts" from heaven to the faithful (Eph. 4:8-11). Although not specifically named, the writer of Hebrews recognizes the presence of leaders in the various congregations and reminds his readers to treat them with respect and kindness (Heb. 13:7, 17). From the sociologist's viewpoint, no group can continue to function without leadership.

The Rise of the Clergy

A study of the history of the church soon reveals an emerging clergy following the New Testament era. A doctrine of the priesthood arose whose roots were far more closely related to the Old Testament than to the New. Sanctioned and adopted by the Roman Catholic Church, the system of a special class of priests was to dominate Western culture for centuries. The creation of "high office" by the Catholic church helped give rise to many kinds of extravagance and abuse during the Middle Ages. Some of the most powerful figures in a feudal Europe were prelates in the Roman church. Often these men functioned as political princes rather than as servants of the Lord Jesus Christ.

One of the salient points of the Protestant Reformation was a renewed emphasis upon the New Testament doctrine of the "priesthood of believers." Martin Luther sternly renounced the idea that men can impose themselves as "mediators" between God and men and called upon his followers to recognize Jesus Christ as men's only true mediator.

Alexander Campbell strongly denounced the "hireling clergy" during the American frontier days. Many leaders who participated in the Campbell-Stone movement in this country refused to wear the title "Reverend," believing that such an ascription belongs only to God. Campbell felt that Protestantism (in some respects) had strayed from the New Testament concept of a universal priesthood almost as far as Roman Catholicism.

Western culture today is still strongly oriented toward the clergy system. The enlistment and education of clergymen for congregations of various religious groups continues to be a pressing need. Many ministers openly acknowledge themselves as a part of a continuing clerical system. They reserve the right to hold special titles, to wear special dress, to baptize, administer communion, call in the hospital, and perform a variety of functions commonly accepted in society as the work of a clergyman.

Although an increasing number of ministers in America disavow the clergy system, because of the role which our society enforces upon them and the expectations of the congregations, they continue to function in much the same way as their clerical brothers. Merely instructing people in the congregation not to use the title "reverend" does not strike at the root of the problem. An entire process of re-education must take place. A minister who encourages others in the congregation to baptize or to share in the hospital calling may struggle through difficult times if people do not understand. A congregation may even feel a minister is trying to get others to do his work.

Concept of an Equipping Ministry

In the fourth chapter of Ephesians, the apostle Paul leaves very little doubt about the primary role of those who function as leaders in the body of Christ. They are to equip the saints for ministry (v. 11). Unfortunately, many translations have a comma which separates "saints" from "the work of the ministry." This misplaced punctuation has sometimes been referred to as the "fatal comma." Leaving out the comma, the passage reads, "And his gifts were that some should be apostles, some prophets, some evangelists, some pastors and teachers, FOR THE EQUIPMENT OF THE SAINTS FOR THE WORK OF THE MINISTRY . . . ." The work of Christian leadership is then clearly defined as preparing the people of God to minister.

The failure to read the New Testament clearly in regard to "ministry" has led to at least two fundamental errors. The first error is related to the function of what should be the "leadership" or "equipping" ministry. At present, the congregation observes while "the minister" performs his ministry. He becomes the one who preaches, teaches, calls on the sick, visits the new-born, ministers to the bereaved, edits the church paper, takes charge of the worship folder, drops in on backsliders, represents the congregation at civic functions, and (if he has time) seeks the lost.

28

Most congregations have a group of officials chosen by the people who (in many instances) function as intermediaries between the congregation and "the minister." If a minister does well according to the expectations of the congregation and the officials, he is praised for his efforts. If, on the other hand, he performs poorly according to their expectations, he is usually encouraged to minister elsewhere.

Frequently, a misguided concept of the nature of a ministering leadership in the congregation has given many ministers the feeling of being constantly on trial. The insecurity of their position often involves them in a power struggle in order to insure their leadership. Members of the congregation who judge their leadership poorly sometimes become a threat which leads a minister into a protective and sometimes a political stance in congregational life. Because many ministers have misunderstood the nature of their own ministry. often frustration and defeat become the prevailing mood.

Some ministers frankly look upon themselves as functioning as a type of corporation executive. Their methods would be perfectly acceptable in the world of big business. Believing strongly in the rights of their own leadership, they begin to make their influence felt in all areas of congregational life even to the color of paint on sanctuary walls or a particular make of organ. The refusal by some of the congregation to accept their prevailing influence is tantamount to a rejection of their personal leadership.

The second fundamental error is related to the scope of the leadership ministry. "The minister" is employed primarily to minister to the congregation. His salary comes from the congregation. The members of a congregation have certain expectations of their minister, most of which are related to the spiritual needs of the congregation. If a minister fails to call upon a member of the congregation who is in the hospital, he may be sternly reminded of his failure. On the other hand, he may repeatedly pass the home of a poor family with several children attending no Sunday School and be censured by no one.

Because the pressure points upon a minister are from within the congregation, he may have the genuine heart of an evangelist and be almost incapable of finding the added time to express his concern for the lost. Many ministers have come to feel, consequently, that the care of a congregation actually hinders the work of evangelism.

Working Through the Problem

The problem of ministry today will never be solved merely by clinging more doggedly to the *status quo*. It will be resolved only as those who

who are truly interested in the growth of the kingdom of God make a renewed study of the New Testament concept of ministry and take remedial steps.

The minister who desires to follow the apostolic tradition should see himself as an "equipper" of others to minister. He can develop a pastoring ministry by training others to call on the sick and visit the bereaved. He can develop an evangelistic ministry by visiting the homes of the lost with those from the congregation who have an evangelistic concern. He can encourage a ministry of benevolence by helping to discover avenues whereby the congregation feeds the hungry, clothes the naked, welcomes the stranger, and visits the prisoners (Matt. 25:31f).

If a congregation takes the New Testament idea of ministry seriously, one can no longer speak of a congregation and the minister but rather of a ministering-congregation. Since congregational participation in ministry is not simply a matter of sitting in a prescribed number of worship services, a congregation which formerly had three hundred members with one minister now has ideally three-hundred ministers.

Working through problems relating to ministry must not be looked upon as merely an academic exercise. The future of millions of persons around the globe is dependent upon the correct solutions being found. Less than one per cent of the American Christians are clergymen leaving over 99 per cent who are non-clergy. Only as the church is mobilized in its entirety can one begin to think of evangelizing the three out of four homes in this country which constitute a mission field. Furthermore, unless our current pattern of ministry is changed, how does one think of reaching two billion unreached? At the present time, over 40 million Americans are worshipping God on Sunday. What would happen in this nation if these 40 million became ministers? What would happen in our world?

Our forefathers coined the slogan, "The Evangelization of the World in This Generation." Contrary to popular understanding, they did not see their task as being accomplished once and for all. They simply realized that the present Christian task force is the only one which will ever have the opportunity of reaching the existing multitudes with the gospel.

An exploding population makes it imperative that Christians face up to the fact that millions will continue to die in their sins unless congregations change their ways. The harvest is still plentiful and the laborers still few (Matt. 9:35-38). Only as the number of harvesters is dramatically increased can we begin to think of reaching a rapidly multiplying harvest.

IV

THE PRINCIPLE OF THE TAUGHT TEACHING

Origin of the Sunday School

The Sunday School has become such an accepted feature of American congregational life that often little consideration is given to its origin. In 1780, Robert Raikes, an English philanthropist, organized a Sunday School for the poor children of Gloucester, England. Later he secured the co-operation of Thomas Stock, a minister. Before the passing of the child labor laws in England, many children were working six days a week. The average working day was from twelve to sixteen hours. Raikes and his friends wanted to do something about this deplorable situation. Their answer was to start a school which met on Sunday. The original Sunday Schools had a wider curriculum than the Bible. They also included subjects which were normally taught in schools sponsored by the government.

Suspicious of all innovations, especially from England, American ministers regarded the

Sunday School as an instrument of the devil for many years. The idea of a Sunday School associated with the Sunday morning services of the congregation gradually gained in popularity, especially as the revivalism of the frontier began to be replaced by a view of Christian nurture.

It is extremely easy to point to the significance of teaching from a Biblical viewpoint. The Old Testament abounds with scriptures indicating the importance of instruction in the home. Jesus may be viewed as the supreme Teacher. The Great Commission twice mentions teaching. ACTS is an extension of "all that Jesus began to do and teach" (1:1). Teachers figure prominently in the early church (cp. Acts 13:1; Eph. 4:11). Paul admonishes Timothy to "be unfailing in patience and teaching" (II Tim. 4:2). He instructs fathers to bring up their children "in the discipline and instruction of the Lord" (Eph. 6:4). Christian educators brought these scriptures to bear upon the need for Christian teaching and helped launch Sunday Schools all across North America.

As the idea of Sunday Schools began to grow, Sunday School associations were formed where the latest ideas could be exchanged. Seminaries began to add departments of "Christian Education." Religious journals were begun which dealt almost exclusively with lesson materials and the promotion of Christian education. Gradually some schools began to employ educational techniques being utilized in public education and follow a grading system.

A Strange School

Looking back, the Sunday School has turned out to be a rather strange school. Sometimes organized higgledy-piggledy, the names of the classes themselves have often been misleading. I remember well a congregation where great-grandparents regularly attended a "young married couples" class. My efforts to change the name of the class to something more descriptive resulted in wounded feelings. Rivalry between classes often surfaces when a building program provides new classrooms. Some classes build such strong institutional loyalty to the class that frequently a congregational overview is slighted. I am aware of one class which bought its own dishes and silverware and kept them in a locked cupboard in the fellowship hall. Other classes were not welcome to use these utensils.

Perhaps strangest of all is not the fact that classes meeting in the name of Christ develop selfish institutional loyalties but rather the idea that the majority of those attending Sunday School never graduate. Thousands of congregations have members who have been faithfully attending as pupils for fifty years! Frequently, ornamental pins are distributed to the members for their faithfulness. It seldom occurs to the teachers or the pupils that one purpose of a school is to produce teachers of others. Paul reminded Timothy that he was to pass on the teaching which he had received (II Tim. 2:2). The writer of Hebrews is distressed because his readers have not grown to be teachers (5:12). Adult Sunday School classes in North America are filled with hundreds of thousands of potential teachers who have yet to teach their first lesson.

Elders in the New Testament are commissioned to be capable teachers (I Tim. 3:2). The question may be raised regarding an elder who has a speech defect or who has some other physical difficulty. The requirement to teach, it seems to me, cannot serve as a blanket command but does reflect the expectations in the early church toward those who lead in the congregation. Others may point to the fact that Paul says "some" are gifts by Christ as teachers in the church (Eph. 4:11). The relative nature of the term "some," however, makes this word ambiguous. It is also true that James cautions against the idea of rushing into teaching without self-examination (James 3:1). These references and others must be considered and heeded but they cannot be used to justify the non-teaching thousands in American congregations.

Multiplying Classes

Research in growing Sunday Schools has indicated that in this kind of voluntary association, one of the keys to expansion is the constant multiplication of classes. It is especially important to keep classes small for pupils of public school age. Students from underprivileged areas may require an even lower teacher-to-pupil ratio.

Some experts in the Sunday School say that no class up through the twelfth grade should be allowed to increase to more than ten pupils. A further idea is to provide a team teacher with every class (an idea which also has merit on the adult level). The second individual would be a "teacher" in every sense of the word—not just a "scissors-and-paste" person. Both teachers would scour the community for those pupils who belonged in the age-group they are teaching. As soon as the class passes ten, each teacher takes five pupils, adds another team teacher, and rebuilds to ten and divides again. Many Sunday Schools across the land have made extremely rapid gains by employing this simple method.

Since the multiplication of classes requires the multiplication of teachers, the bottleneck often comes at this point. Many congregations are chronically short of teachers. Here is the place where the purpose of the Sunday School needs to be re-examined. Many Sunday Schools are not graduating teachers in large numbers because they have never been designed to graduate teachers. Thousands of adults in Sunday School classes (high school students must not be overlooked either) have never been challenged with the idea of teaching. Instead, the class roll is checked year after year with repeated admonitions to be "faithful to Sunday School."

Adults in the Sunday School who are asked to teach, frequently reply, "I'm sorry, but I simply do not feel I know enough." Many are undoubtedly very sincere in their answer. It could be, however, that they are underestimating their own reservoir of information. Many Christian adults in this country have attended at least three religious gatherings (Sunday A.M. and P.M. and Wednesday night) totaling four hours of religious services every week. This figure does not include evangelistic meetings, area rallies, or other special services. By the time these adults are forty, they have been in a total of 8,320 hours of religious services. By contrast, the university student, graduating after four years, has spent 2,176 hours in the classroom.

It is difficult to believe that an individual of average intelligence with a total of over 8,000 hours in religious services is incapable of teaching someone else at least the fundamentals of the

Christian faith. Furthermore, all kinds of wonderful Sunday School helps are available today for a willing teacher. Lesson helps and outlines have been carefully prepared by experienced teachers. What is required most is simply a willingness to begin and an eagerness to keep learning.

A Demonstration of Love

It has become popular in our time to demonstrate for a particular cause. What finer demonstration of Christian love could be made by the church than to increase its teaching force by the thousands. One couple I know decided after many hours of self-examination to take the idea of teaching seriously. They let their Sunday School teacher know about their plans. He was actually a little piqued at them because it would mean a drop in his class attendance at a time when he was in a contest with another class. This couple decided they could work with children in the fourth grade. They approached the leaders in the Sunday School for a classroom. After getting a list of all fourth graders from the office of the public school, they began to call systematically. They found three out of every four pupils not attending any Sunday School. Together, they began to reach fourth-graders for Christ by the dozens.

This illustration needs to be multiplied by a million and more. Suppose those individuals who are willing to be teachers would begin to look for the opportunity of telling boys and girls in their community about Jesus Christ. What could happen in North America, if a million new classes a year could be formed. These classes, as well as existing ones, could very well follow the pattern of grading already set by the public school system. These outside of Sunday School circles are unfamiliar with the special terms which are employed by Christian educators. If you ask an unchurched fourth grader if he wants to be in a fourth-grade Sunday School class, however, he understands immediately his position.

A reference has been made earlier to the long list of available helps for a teacher. Colorful Sunday School literature can be purchased in hundreds of Bible book stores. Of course, the Bible itself as a textbook must not be overlooked. Paperback editions of the Bible in today's English are usually very inexpensive. With these helps and a prayerful interest in every pupil, the loving Sunday School teacher may be responsible for changing the lives of hundreds.

Teaching a Sunday School class may be an expression of the Christian ministry in one of its finest dimensions. One can point to Jesus as the teacher who changed the lives of eleven men who changed the world. Early impressions are lasting impressions. The Sunday School teacher who loves children, especially those children who come from loveless homes, can make a complete difference in their lives. Many of us can point to a Sunday School teacher or teachers in our own lives who helped to give us a better understanding of the gospel. Where might we be today were it not for their influence in our lives? Do any of us have the right to keep back from others that greatest of all gifts, the gospel, which has come to us?

The current situation in the Sunday School in relation to the world need could be compared to a raging epidemic of diptheria while classes of physicians learn again and again how to give innoculations. Faced with an epidemic of sinful and broken lives in America, members of the Sunday School are learning again and again that Jesus Christ saves us from sin. If the greatest malady of our nation is spiritual sickness which can only be cured by the Great Physician, then surely the time is now for Christians to let others know about Him who redeems us.

Spiritual Gain for the Teacher

A well-known proverb states that what we give to bless the lives of others comes back to bless our own. Faithful teachers often point to their own beginning days in teaching as the time their knowledge of the Bible began to increase.

Simply sitting in a Sunday School class year after year can actually have injurious spiritual results. Students have the tendency to confuse the hearing of the lesson with doing what the lesson implies. Jesus gave ample warning about this situation in the parable of the Two Builders (Matt. 7:24-27).

On the other hand, the individual who decides to become a teacher for Jesus Christ may expect some revolutionary changes. It has been proven through studies in the Sunday School that men make some of the best teachers for pre-school age. They are loved by their pupils and especially by the girls. One congregational leader and his wife decided to graduate from their adult class and work with the pre-school department. The increase in their own measure of Christian joy was dramatically multiplied when they began to see the fascination which the gospel has for young lives.

THE PRINCIPLE OF MULTIPLYING CONGREGATIONS

From Rural to Urban

One well-known expert in church growth said recently that we need fifty-thousand new congregations in the United States and Canada—tomorrow! The great majority of these congregations should be in the urban areas since America is now predominantly an urban nation. A few statistics are very revealing. In 1790, this nation was approxinately 20 per cent urban and 80 per cent rural. Today, these figures are almost reversed. The process of urbanization has dramatically increased during the past few decades. Between 1940 and 1968 the size of the average American farm increased from 167 acres to 369 acres while farm population decreased from thirty million to ten million during the same era. The drop is not so dramatic, however, in rural population as a whole. Total rural population declined six million between 1950 and 1960.

The establishment of new congregations in urban areas has not kept pace with the rate of urbanization. Religion followed the frontier as it swept westward across this country. In tens of thousands of hamlets and villages as well as in the open country, new congregations were established. For well over a century, the congregations "in the wildwood" radiated their influence across the land.

Today, many small American towns are caught in shifting tides of population. The closed stores in the business districts are mute testimony to the prosperity of previous days. Young people leave the community as soon as they graduate from high school. Very few new houses are being built. Schools are consolidated in an effort to keep pace with modern educational methods. It soon becomes apparent, even to the most casual observer, that a community is dying.

The church buildings in a dying or static community may represent the investment of hundreds of thousands of dollars. During the post-World War II boom in American church attendance, many congregations erected very fine houses of worship or completely remodeled existing buildings. More adequate Sunday School facilities were added. Many of these buildings are now only being used at one-third to one-half of capacity. With young couples constantly seeking employment in urban areas, attendance of children in Sunday School sharply declines.

The picture of declining population in rural areas does not necessarily mean stagnation. Some of the most stable Christians in American society live in the rural areas. Survival in agriculture requires wise planning and sound financing. Many Christians in rural areas have giving power which cannot yet be matched by their urban brothers.

Rural congregations are often thriving today in spite of declining populations in rural areas. The automobile (frequently two or three per family) has made transportation a minor item. Rural families have shown a willingness to travel twenty miles or more to participate in an active church. A congregation with a house of worship in the open country can draw worshippers from surrounding towns and villages if it has an aggressive evangelistic program. Denominational barriers are becoming less and less important to Americans. They will worship where they are wanted and where the Bible is still being preached and taught.

Sunday Schools can also grow in rural areas. I know of one dedicated teacher who spent hours each week calling in the homes of children who were not in Sunday School. Then she would arrange to stop by their home on Sunday morning and bring them to the house of God. Many of those children are now grown with Christian families of their own. Some are preaching the gospel in other lands. Her faithfulness will not be unrewarded (John 4:36).

With all that may be said for the possibilities for church growth in the rural areas, it is still true that at the present time, the great potential for multiplying congregations is in the urban areas. Giant strip cities several hundred miles long and often a hundred miles in width are being formed. At the present time, urban populations in the world are expected to double every eleven years and keep on redoubling. It is not unusual for several hundred communities of 5000 or more to form around a central city in a few years. To plant new congregations in each of these communities is one of the greatest evangelistic challenges in Christian history. Urban areas may be referred to as the new frontiers of our time.

Mother and Daughter Congregations

In order to disciple the growing millions living in urban areas, an increasing number of congregations must become interested in motherhood. A congregation whose leadership is sold on planting new congregations can be the mother and grandmother of dozens of congregations. Such an attitude requires a great deal of soul-searching by members of the "mothering" congregation.

As a "staying" member of a congregation, it may not be easy to watch several families leave on a given Sunday in order to establish a new congregation in a strategic part of the city. Those who are leaving are probably among the top giving members of the congregation, both in time and treasure. They may represent a sizeable block of current leadership in the congregation. Others will need to pick up the congregational responsibilities which those who are leaving have laid down in their former congregation.

On the other hand, it is usually not easy for those who are leaving. Across the years, they may have formed vital and active friendships with many members of their previous congregation. Perhaps they have given liberally toward the erection of a commodious house of worship and they must now think in terms of giving generously again for the same cause. They may have enjoyed a position of leadership which may now be lost in the levelling process of a new daughter congregation.

The cost of leaving, however, is often more than compensated for by the joy of pioneering. Charter members of a new congregation often point with pride and thankfulness to the picture of a handful of people who struggled a few years before to start a new congregation. Then they look at the current attendance board which shows how their efforts have been multipled. Many of them have performed functions of Christian service in the new congregation, because of necessity, which they never dreamed they could do. It is also interesting to note the rise of latent leadership in the mothering congregations. With many former congregational leadership posts now vacant, former sitting-type members move into worker roles.

The establishing of daughter congregations by a mother congregation is not without its difficulties. A question often arises regarding the timing of a new congregation. The existing congregation may feel she is not strong enough to give birth to a congregation at this particular time. It has been previously indicated that here is a place where soul-searching must take place. If a congregation is intent upon being the largest in the state or territory, it may never feel strong enough to have spiritual children. Planting new congregations, it has been shown repeatedly, does not usually deter the growth of the mothering congregation. In fact, in many instances, a consistent policy of planting new congregations has increased the concern for the kingdom by the existing congregation to the point that its growth rate has actually increased.

It is essential in the multiplication of new congregations that a daughter share the same unselfish concern of the mother. Sometimes the offspring of a sponsoring congregation began to vie with the other children in attendance and giving. At times, the goal may be to increase to a larger attendance than the mother. If these dubious attitudes are allowed to go unchecked, they can render serious damage to the body of Christ. Instead of a spirit of mutual helpfulness, selfishness and party-spirit reign. The wider view of the kingdom of God is displaced by a narrow and self-seeking view for the local congregation. If the daughter congregations will continue to reproduce themselves, growth in the kingdom will result.

Happy is the congregation that can take a kingdom view regarding its spiritual children. No longer feeling the threat of new congregations, a church can rally with renewed vigor to the cause of evangelism. A larger congregation may have a preaching staff of three or four members. Instead of tying these people to small bits of the worship program, their place can be cheerfully taken by other members of the congregation and those who preach can be sent out each Sunday to meet with a small nucleus of people who are forming a new congregation. Then as Jesus said, "sower and reaper may rejoice together" (John 4:36).

Additional Urban Strategy

It is very possible that one of the best ways for new congregations to be started is by individual response to the Great Commission. Instead of looking for an existing congregation, those who are interested in the growth of the kingdom should be starting new congregations. In one large metropolitan area, a Christian couple opened their home to those in their neighborhood who were seeking Christian teaching and fellowship. Today, a thriving congregation is the result of their concern.

A rediscovery of the home as a place of worship harks back to the numerous household congregations which are mentioned in the New Testament (Rom. 16:5; I Cor. 16:19; Col. 4:15, Philem. 2). Indeed, the early Christians worshipped for nearly three centuries without special church buildings.

Current emphasis upon small Bible study groups and a less formal atmosphere for teaching and worship is making the use of the home even more desirable. The family room in many American homes can seat almost as many people (sometimes more) as the small rural church buildings erected before the turn of the century. Christians moving to an urban area may even choose a home in an unchurched community with the idea of establishing a congregation there.

In many metropolitan areas, evangelizing fellowships have been formed with the express purpose of developing new congregations. Many of these fellowships have been instrumental in establishing dozens of congregations. They have been extremely valuable in urban areas. For the most part, however, these evangelizing fellowships work along the lines of addition. They add a congregation this year and add another congregation the next. Existing congregations sometimes adopt the attitude that their gifts to the evangelizing agency take care of their responsibility. Only as congregations take church planting initiative along with the evangelizing agency can true multiplication of congregations take place.

High-caliber Christian personnel often minister with a printing firm or a benevolent institution. The usual pattern is for these individuals to place their membership in a nearby congregation which may already have an abundance of leadership. Their presence in the congregation may even stifle the initiative of those who are less gifted and less highly educated. If such an institution is near a metropolitan area, how much more beneficial to the kingdom it would be if those who are preaching-teaching type leaders would help to start new congregations around the city. As the new work developed beyond their capacity to keep up with it, they could turn their positions of leadership over to others and begin elsewhere.

Potential in a Christian College

A Christian college in an area may have a strong influence in planting new congregations. Paul seems to have had a walking college with him most of the time. Luke mentions Timothy, Erastus, Sopater, Aristarchus, Secundus, Gaius, Tychicus, Trophimus, and himself (Acts 19:22; 20:4-5). After serving with Paul in a program of in-service training, Paul dispatched his helpers to various needy areas. He sent Timothy to Corinth (I Cor. 4:17) and left Titus in Crete which was evidently a difficult field (Titus 1:5).

The staff of a Christian college usually includes a number of career ministers. Their experienced hand may be a great help in guiding a new congregation during its period of infancy. Students in the college may find a practical application for their learning by serving as census-takers, callers, hospital visitors, musicians, preachers, teachers, youth leaders and in a myriad other ways. Summers may provide an opportunity for overseas ministries. Several hundred new congregations could result from the activity of those associated with a Christian educational institution.

The City and the New Testament

The call for urban evangelism is no innovation in the Christian gospel. The gospel went in New Testament times to the city and then to the surrounding rural areas. Paul evidently viewed Antioch of Syria, Antioch of Pisidia, Ephesus, Philippi, Thessalonica, Corinth, Athens, Rome and other metropolitan areas as evangelizing centers. From these radiating points, the gospel could penetrate an entire region (I Thess. 1:6-8).

American cities should be viewed today as a great harvest field for the gospel. Spiritual resources must be poured in for their regeneration. To fail in the cities is to fail with the majority of people now living in this nation.

VI

THE PRINCIPLE OF THE KINGDOM OF GOD ABOVE THE INSTITUTION

Institutions Versus Institutionalism

Society cannot exist without certain basic institutions. Patterns for the family, educational procedures, occupational opportunities, forms of government, and various types of religious expressions are all a part of the institutions of any culture. Among those nations which are highly industrial, the institutional life of society becomes increasingly complex.

The word "institution" itself means basically "arrangement," "custom," or "instruction." The concept is concerned with the organized aspects of a stable society. Without some kind of institutional life, a society degenerates into anarchy and chaos, causing the death of the society itself.

Every Christian congregation exists as an institution which operates on principles of arrangement and instruction. Worship and study at set times become a part of its institutional life. The

54

fact that Paul could meet with various groups of Christians in different cities reflects some type of common arrangement (cp. Acts 20:7). Many of the early Christians were reared in the synagogue, an important institution in Jewish life. Consequently, little difficulty was presented in the transition to a Christian congregation, which also had an orderly way of public religious expression. The various household congregations in the New Testament were also manifestations of institutional life.

The difficulty arises, not with the concept of institutions, but with the idea of "institutionalism." This latter word reflects an excessive dependence upon institutions with overtones of standardization and regimentation. It can be freely stated that the New Testament does not sanction institutionalism.

The New Testament breathes the spirit of freedom, which is the very opposite of conventionality and regimentation. Paul informs the Corinthians that "where the spirit of the Lord is, there is freedom" (II Cor. 3:17). He is determined that the Galatians should protect their freedom in Christ against the institutionalizing Judaizers who want to impose a stifling kind of legalism upon young Christians (Gal. 5:1).

The ministry of Jesus breathes an atmosphere of religious freedom (Mark 7:1-7). Jesus disregarded many of the Jewish religious traditions, which opened him to the fanatical hatred of the Pharisees (Mark 2:23-3:6). It was, indeed, the leaders of institutional religion who brought about his crucifixion.

No one who reads the New Testament diligently should quarrel with the idea of the congregation as an institution. He has every right, however, to be suspicious of an institutionalism which denies a spirit of freedom and reflects selfishness on the part of the institution. Institutions are to be servants of a larger cause, and when they turn inward and serve only themselves, then they have denied the basis for their existence. Particularly is this statement true for the congregation, whose very purpose for existence is to serve the advancement of the kingdom.

The Congregation As a Serving Institution

When does a congregation lapse into institutionalism? Of course, it is difficult to pinpoint degrees of change, but it may be stated that a congregation is guilty of institutionalism when its primary function becomes the service of itself rather than the gospel of Christ. Institutionalism may be reflected in a calling program. One minister told a group of visitation callers to ignore those who were moving out of the community "since they will not be any help to our church." Such an incident is not an isolated one. By way of contrast, another congregation located in a great American seaport keeps in touch with service men moving in and out of their community. Although their attendance in worship shows no great increase over a ten year period, this congregation has had a tremendous ministry for Christ in a transient area. Here is a congregation which is seeking first the kingdom of God (Matt. 6:33).

A congregation which practices a ministry to produce believers cannot think of families moving away as "losing members." It is true that the attendance of these families in that place of worship will no longer be reflected in the "attendance and offering" figures there. It is also true, however, that if these families serve Christ wherever they are, they are a part of the ministry of their previous congregation. Moving into an area which is unchurched, a family may start a home Bible study or a small weekly meeting in a public building which may be the beginning of a new congregation. Their work, then, becomes a part of the kingdom-extension.

Sometimes institutionalism tends to prevent the planting of new congregations. A church may think of its goal as "having the largest number of people possible who can gather in one congregation." This attitude often overlooks outlying areas where additional congregations would reach more people for Christ. Such a statement is in no way intended to reflect upon the power and influence of the large congregation. A congregation of 1000 people or more has unquestionably a larger potential than a congregation of 100. It is not without significance that the congregation in Jerusalem began with 3000 plus members. By the same token, however, if the early Christians had not spread out from Jerusalem, taking the gospel with them and establishing congregations as they went, there may have never been Christians in America to discuss this point.

The Individual and the Congregation

The basic unit of the congregation is the individual. It is the religious needs of the individual which the congregation should serve. Jesus sharply reminded the Pharisees that "the Sabbath was made for man, not man for the Sabbath" (Mark 3:27). We may make a contemporary application of the verse by reminding ourselves that Jesus established the church for the sake of individuals and not individuals for the sake of the church.

Members of a congregation who attend its services Sunday after Sunday may develop the feeling that they are being depersonalized. With very little opportunity for expression, except to occupy a pew at stated hours, they may think that individuals are wanted for religious services rather than services for individuals. A congregation may build a larger house of worship and have its leaders more concerned about keeping it filled than about the spiritual needs of individuals.

It is no secret that the growing congregations today are those which are most adequately fulfilling personal needs. A high school boy who will not attend a class of thirty may gladly come to a class of five, where he feels he counts as an individual. A congregation which emphasizes small study groups in homes often has renewed interest in worship on Sunday morning. In an age of depersonalization, it is imperative that the congregation keep its emphasis upon the individual. The business world is rediscovering the importance of the individual. It remains to be seen whether the church can read the signs of the times.

Congregational growth does not usually occur when sought as an end within itself but as a by-product of the serving of a congregation. Most individuals do not want to be simply another digit on a congregational attendance board. They are not interested in moving up another notch in the attendance ranks of religious journals. They do want to be wanted for their own sake. Members of a congregation who go throughout the community with love in their hearts for individuals will usually

strike a responsive chord in others. Such a concern must not be limited by any color bar or social
standing. It must be extended to people as people
who have been created in the image of God.

Congregations sometimes make a sad mistake.
They may think that a more adequate house of worship can serve as a substitute for individual concern. Legion are the congregations which have felt
that a new church building would inspire a great
increase in attendance. No house of worship, no
matter how attractive, can take the place of love
and fellowship. Many of the cathedrals in Europe,
with some of the most beautiful church architecture
in the world, are virtually empty today. The congregation which is depending largely upon a building to increase attendance will be sadly dis-
appointed. Such statements are not at all intended
to minimize the importance of church buildings.
It is a matter of gaining the proper perspective.
Viewed as a tool in God's harvest field (as a
farmer might view a new farm implement) they can
be an important factor in the growth of the congregation.

The Congregation and Global Concern

Perhaps at no point does a congregation
reveal its institutionalism or lack of it than in the
area of a global witness by the congregation. The

Great Commission given by Jesus involves every congregation interested in being a church of Christ in a world-wide concern. The monies given by a congregation to provide for a more adequate house of worship can have a tinge of selfishness, since it is usually the members themselves who benefit from the use of the building.

Mission work, of course, does not necessarily involve an overseas project. A need for a new congregation on the other side of a city may be justifiably called a missionary project. It is still true, however, that some of the greatest needs in evangelism are outside the North American continent. Hundreds of thousands of communities around the world have still never heard the gospel of Christ. The great metropolitan areas of the world are virtually unevangelized.

Many congregations today are calling a minister at home and a minister abroad. They provide for the physical needs of a man and his family who are engaged in world evangelism. As time goes on, they seek to enlarge their staff of overseas ministers. It is not unknown for one American congregation to support as many as 300 overseas missionaries! Such enthusiasm for the cause of the gospel world-wide is the very opposite of that of being a congregation which seeks to serve primarily itself.

A congregation, however, may still need to be reminded that the Great Commission begins at home. Jesus instructed the early disciples to begin in Jerusalem (Acts 1:8). Our Jerusalem may be the next-door neighbor. Certainly it would include our own communities. One man may be perfectly willing to give money for the cause of world-wide evangelism, but reluctant to be a witness for Christ where he is. The idea of "sending" does not negate the idea of our own participation in the cause of evangelism.

Many congregations express their concern for others through the support of serving institutions. Most religious bodies sponsor educational and benevolent institutions which in turn serve the needs of others. Consequently, a college or seminary which prepares career workers in the kingdom may be one avenue used by a congregation to express its global concern. A congregation may support a religious writer and his family because he is involved in carrying the gospel to others by means of the printed word.

The congregation which exists for others will find the need constantly outstretching its ability to serve. It may feel that it offers only a clamshell to dip out the ocean. Yet, the combined abilities of thousands of congregations in North America are inestimable. No greater force may be found in the universe today. More powerful than the force of a hundred hydrogen bombs is the spiritual power which is latent today in the American congregations. The unleasing of that power is dependent upon the willingness of each congregation to be a servant of Jesus Christ in the world. Freed from complacency and self-seeking, the genuinely serving congregation will find new vistas of spiritual life. It will find that congregations, like individuals, truly find their lives when they lose them (Luke 9:24).

VII

APPLYING PRINCIPLES OF CHURCH GROWTH
IN THE CONGREGATION

Action Versus Theory

The preceding pages of this book have dealt primarily with some basic principles of church growth. No set of principles can help the congregation which basks in mire of complacency. For those congregations who take the global evangelizing commissions of Jesus seriously, however, the question of growth involves a willingness to conduct a self-examination. Once a congregation has decided upon a theory of action, to fail to act can lead to pessimism and despair. A well-known maxim runs, "Impression without expression leads to depression."

A problem is caused by the habit of confusing theory with action. Listening to a stirring sermon on the deepening spiritual value of a devout prayer life will not accomplish anything until one prays. A course of study on evangelism must not

64

be confused with evangelizing. Perhaps the most difficult problem of all is moving the average congregation from theory to action.

Placing a premium upon action does not nullify the importance of good theory. Many congregations are not going to make significant gains in evangelism until they rethink their basic situation. Fuzzy thinking can only lead to faulty action.

The mandate to most of us today in evangelism is to think about the way we think, God helping us. Then we must move out of the theoretical stage into effective action.

Spontaneous and Planned evangelism

Several methods of evangelism practiced by Jesus are easily traced in the gospels. One method could be called "spontaneous." Weary from his travels one day, Jesus rested at Jacob's well. There he met a Samaritan woman with a scarlet past who had come to draw water. The Lord spoke to her about the water of life. Because of her enthusiasm, an entire village was converted (John 4:42).

Passing through Jericho, Jesus spotted little Zaccheus lodged in a sycamore tree. Jesus promptly invited himself to his home and won another convert (Luke 19:9). The gospel writers take account of numerous incidents in the ministry of Jesus in which he used a spontaneous situation to bring the good news of the kingdom to others.

It has been said that the average American comes into direct contact with at least thirty different people every day. These contacts would include the filling station attendant, check-out personnel in the super market, post office employees, and a host of others. A congregation with two-hundred members could theoretically make forty-two thousand approaches for the gospel every week! Some of these contacts over a week's time would, of course, involve the same people.

As indicated previously, Jesus also followed a "planned" method of evangelism. He sent out the twelve, two by two, on missionary journeys in Galilee and Judea. He also sent out seventy others "into every town and village" (Luke 10:2). We can assume different assignments for each team to eliminate the possibility of all of them going to the same town.

A congregation which hopes to reach every unchurched person in the community for Christ simply cannot rely on spontaneous evangelism alone. Those who live within the proximity of a congregation's house of worship will probably not be reached at all unless that congregation makes a planned effort. Many times this endeavor involves a house-to-house plan such as Paul seems to have followed in Ephesus (Acts 20:20-21).

Just as the physician gathers information about the physical condition of someone he is trying to help, so the congregation must gather information relating to the spiritual background of people. Names, family ties, vocations, ethnic and racial groupings, are extremely important. Jesus dealt with each person according to his background. Contrast, for example, his treatment of Nicodemus with the woman at Jacob's well.

Our Lord said he came "to seek and save the lost" (Luke 19:10). There is no point in arguing the fact that many will be lost unless they are actively sought. Some church members are reluctant to call on others for Christ because of what they phrase, "a breach of privacy." Those who intend to keep their privacy, of course, can always do so. Meanwhile, there are millions of desperate, lonely people in our world who would welcome the extended hand of Christ's love in their home. Part of the solution is in the way we seek people. If we seek them to extend the influence of our institutions, they will be unconcerned. They must be sought purely, for their own sakes, by those who have the concern of Christ.

From "Come" to "Go" Structures

The congregation which moves from being primarily characterized by a "come-structure" to one which also combines the structure of "going" does not usually make the transition in a matter of a few weeks. Old habit patterns are not easily dissolved. The church member who feels comfortable attending a stated number of religious services every week suddenly feels the impingement of a larger call. How does a congregation deal with a new awareness of its responsibility to the lost?

A church board meeting may be a good place to begin discussing some priorities in congregational life. What are the opportunities for the congregation to develop its own inner spiritual life and at the same time to be constantly reaching out to others? Several class sessions on Sunday morning could be devoted to the theme, "How can we help to fulfill the Great Commission more effectively?" A Sunday night worship-type service could become an open forum for several weeks making it possible for the members of the congregation to speak freely about their own fears and convictions.

Suppose a congregation, with repentance for past failures and new resolve for the future, decides to become a genuinely seeking congregation. What then? If the gospel is to be shared with others on a person-to-person basis, how is this goal to be realized?

Consider the follower of Christ who has never shared his faith with an outsider and you will be thinking of the majority of church members in America today. Suppose this person decides with God's help to become an active witness in the kingdom. To start this individual down a row of homes by himself to bear witness for Christ would probably result in a fine resolve turned to a disaster.

Many congregations already have a few individuals who are trained callers. Here is the place where those who are experienced need to educate the inexperienced. Jesus followed a similar practice with the disciples.

Ground rules such as being kind, courteous, and friendly must, of course, be in the back of the caller's mind. Much more is involved, however, than simply being gracious. For the most part, telling the gospel to others involves the teller in circumstances as varied as the different hearers. By working with a trained caller, the fledgling learns to adapt to the various situations.

Contrary to the usual view, under the right circumstances, three people sent on one call are not too many. An experienced caller can train two others as he calls in homes and thereby help multiply the number of laborers for the harvest who are always few (Matt. 9:37).

The Personal Religious Testimony

Some religious groups are fearful of personal testimony in religion and consequently downplay its importance. Such a view is usually unwarranted. The apostle Paul does not hesitate to use personal testimony in his presentation of the gospel (cf. Acts 24:10f; 26:2f).

I have gone house-to-house in major American cities and simply identified myself and my calling companion as being from the _____ congregation. If we are invited inside, the conversation usually includes a personal testimony regarding the meaning which Jesus Christ holds for my companion and me. Such a procedure is natural and informal. It does not require a college degree in Bible, although all Scriptural information is helpful. It is personal and direct. It focusses attention upon the saving power of Jesus Christ in the life of an individual, rather than upon the activities of a particular congregation.

Telling-the-gospel-type calls should naturally be considered. The love of God, man as a sinner, Jesus Christ as Savior, and the abundant life in Christ must be included in a gospel presentation.

Here is the place where the clear teaching of the Scriptures can be brought to bear. The discussion may lead to a consideration of the authenticity of the Bible. Most Christians know more than they realize. They can make this type of call when given coaching and instruction.

Preparing for Results

Something wonderful usually happens when the members of a congregation begin systematically to seek the lost for Christ. People will respond. Some congregations are amazed when they see the results of a genuine effort to share the love of Christ with others.

What does a congregation do with three or five or ten different people who come to Christ each week? "In the front door and out the back door" is a well-known quotation in Christian circles. It should be noted, however, that very few people have any intention of going out the back door when they come in the front. Much of the blame for this loss can be attached to a congregation which simply failed in mothering new babes in Christ.

In his Great Commission, Jesus told us to (1) teach (2) baptize (3) teach. Classes for new members on vital Christian topics are extremely important. Now is the time also to impress upon

71

the new convert that Christ expects him to share his faith. Perhaps nothing is more exciting in the Christian congregation than for new believers to be out telling others the good news a few weeks after their own conversion.

The failure to encourage new Christians to witness is one of the greatest sins of the church. Because churches are afraid to put young Christians in positions of leadership (indeed, the Scripture does give us warning), the new member embarks merely upon a weekly program of attending public worship services. Impression continues but expression is lacking. After several years, the light of evangelistic faith which once burned brightly is only a dim flicker.

Some will turn away from the gospel in spite of all the efforts at conservation. Jesus lost Judas. Paul failed with Demas (II Tim. 4:10). Peter speaks of those who "wallow in the mire" again (II Peter 2:22). To see someone you love going back into the world of sin is a heart breaking experience. The vision of faith is often blurred because of the "lust of the eyes" (I John 2:16).

The Joys of a Growing Congregation

For the most part, it is safe to say that the seeking and teaching congregation in America will be a growing congregation. As a baby brings joy to the home, so those who are new in Christ bring an added sense of joy in the fellowship of believers. Freed from past days of stagnation, the congregation which is filled with new lives offers a constant challenge to those in leadership to provide additional teachers and classes. Such a congregation cannot embark on a once-for-all building program. New classrooms and worship facilities must constantly be provided to meet changing needs.

What greater happiness could a congregation possess than to know it is being used by God to reach out to those whom he loves (John 3:16). Watching family after family come to the Savior and seeing him being "formed" in each life are inexpressible joys (Gal. 4:19). While others reap the grim harvest of carnality (Gal. 5:19-21), the new Christian is blessed by the "fruit of the Spirit" (Gal. 5:22-24).

What could bring greater satisfaction to the heart of a pulpit minister than to realize he is having a part in helping to snatch lives from the jaws of eternal death? What could give a church board meeting more of an atmosphere of seriousness and reverence than to know their wrong decisions and frivolity may mean a soul forever lost?

73

Those who are working daily in the harvest have little time for quibbling about the faults of others. Rejoicing in the work of the kingdom, their time is spent in encouraging other harvesters. Every day they ask God to help them to be better prepared themselves.

Conclusion

The new birth of our world lies within the potential of the Christian congregations which encircle the globe. The hand of the Lord is not shortened. Divine power has always been available for the asking. God has not left us without the resources for our task. Christ continues to knock at the door of our hearts. He still watches for his kingdom to come on earth as it is in heaven.

STUDY SECTION:

TOPICS FOR DISCUSSION

NOTES

Chapter I

CHURCH GROWTH AND
THE NEW TESTAMENT CONGREGATIONS

1. Why is the resurrection of Jesus Christ so vital to the Christian faith?

2. How would you answer the skeptic who stated that in all likelihood, the disciples made up the story about the resurrection?

3. Why is the rapid growth during the New Testament era such a phenomenon?

4. How does one account for the surprising growth of the early church?

5. Why is it hazardous to idealize the congregations of the New Testament?

6. How does a congregation continue to reach the lost in spite of obvious imperfections?

7. What should a congregation do about its own internal difficulties?

NOTES

Chapter II

THE PRINCIPLE OF GATHERING AND SCATTERING

1. What basic plan did Jesus follow in evangelizing?
2. Why did Jesus send out the twelve and the seventy?
3. What does Luke tell us in Acts about worship in the early church?
4. Why is Acts 8:4 important in a New Testament study of church growth?
5. What are the perils to evangelism in a "come-type" congregational life?
6. How does a congregation become too busy to evangelize?
7. What is meant by the "gathering-scattering" pattern?
8. What are some ways by which a congregation which has traditionally been turned inward begins to turn outward?

NOTES

Chapter III

THE PRINCIPLE OF THE
MINISTRY OF ALL BELIEVERS

1. Discuss the New Testament concept of the ministry of believers.

2. Discuss the rise of the clergy.

3. What happens to the ministry of believers when a congregation follows a clergy system?

4. Why do "the minister" and the "church officials" sometimes pose a threat to each other?

5. What are some ways a congregation can begin to bring back the ministry of believers?

6. Why is it so important that the problem of ministry be solved as quickly as possible?

7. What is the "equipping concept" of the ministry?

NOTES

Chapter IV

THE PRINCIPLE OF THE TAUGHT TEACHING

1. Discuss the origin of the Sunday School.
2. Why can the Sunday School be called a "strange school"?
3. Why is the average Sunday School in chronic need of more teachers?
4. Discuss the multiplication of classes.
5. What are some traditional objections to people in adult classes for people who are not teaching?
6. What does the New Testament say in regard to elders teaching?
7. What changes often take place in the life of a Sunday School class member who becomes a teacher?

NOTES

Chapter V

THE PRINCIPLE
OF MULTIPLYING CONGREGATIONS

1. Discuss the impact of urbanization in America in its relationship to the total church.

2. Why has the church been slow in facing the new social climate which urbanization forces upon the church?

3. Does declining population in rural areas necessarily mean religious stagnation?

4. Why is it important to multiply congregations, especially in the urban areas?

5. List some hindrances to the multiplication of congregations?

6. Discuss the idea that a "heresy" may be a perfectly sound doctrine which has been neglected for a generation.

NOTES

Chapter VI

THE PRINCIPLE OF THE KINGDOM OF GOD
ABOVE THE INSTITUTION

1. How would you deal with the individual who said he was opposed to the institutional church?

2. Why is it so easy for institutions to become selfish?

3. Discuss the idea of the congregation as a serving institution.

4. Why does institutionalism in a congregation sometimes prevent the establishing of new congregations?

5. What are some of the ways by which a congregation may be challenged to see the larger view of the kingdom of God?

6. Why must the needs of individuals remain at the focal point of congregational concern?

NOTES

Chapter VII

APPLYING PRINCIPLES OF CHURCH GROWTH IN THE CONGREGATIONS

1. Why do congregations sometimes become depressed?

2. How can the methods which Jesus followed in evangelizing be utilized today?

3. What are some of the steps which a congregation must take to combine a "come-structure" with a "go-structure"?

4. Does personal religious testimony have a place in sharing the gospel with others?

5. Why are many followers of Christ reluctant to share their faith with others?

6. What are some of the joys of the growing congregation?

NOTES

APPENDIX

SUGGESTIONS FOR PLANNED HARVESTING

THE CARE-PROMISE IDEA

SUGGESTIONS FOR PLANNED HARVESTING
FOR CHRIST
Matthew 9:35-38

1. DESIGNATE A TIME

Many Christians will simply allow other important activities to take the place of soul-winning unless a particular slice of time is designated for that purpose. An afternoon or evening each week could be set aside for work in planned harvesting.

2. CHOOSE A PARTNER

Jesus sent the Seventy out two by two. His plan is an important one. Two people can "lean" on each other, help each other, and encourage one another. Experienced callers should constantly be taking new callers with them who in turn can take new callers with them.

3. SELECT A SPIRITUALLY-NEEDY FAMILY OR PERSON

Concentrate first of all upon the lost. One-half of the people in America are not members of any body of Christian believers. They constitute a mission field of over one-hundred million. These people live all around us. They are part of the "world" for whom Jesus died. They are people living without forgiveness of sins and the promise of everlasting life. They often exist in a state of despair and disillusionment. They want someone to love them with the pure love of Christ. It may be a boy or girl living in a ghetto who needs a Sunday School. It may be a suburban family whose interest in materialism has become jaded. It may be a high school or university student who is wondering how he can "make it" in our highly competitive society. It may be an alcoholic or an alienated youth who looks at life through drink and drugs. It may be a new resident looking for a warm family of God. Jesus said he came to "seek and and to save the lost." How do we **find** lost people? They may be people we know through our jobs. They may live down the street from us. Their names may be listed in the office of a building where a church meets for Sunday worship. We must **look** for the lost if we expect to find them.

4. MAKE THE CONTACT

Even the most experienced harvester will have fruitless efforts if he does not go where the harvest is. Plan your place of contact. The home is usually "good talking ground," although some other place may serve just as well. Talk about Jesus Christ. Talk about what he means to you (and your family). Explain why you have chosen "the way." Listen. Listen to what people are saying. Do not just talk past them. Try to determine their philosophy of life and focus the light of the gospel upon it.

5. CALL FOR COMMITMENT
Most calls do not end in commitment, but many calls do. If the one on whom you are calling shows signs of conviction, ask him if he will accept Jesus Christ as Lord and Savior through repentance and obedience (Acts 2:36-38).

6. SUGGEST A CONGREGATION
New Christians sometimes have a very difficult time relating to a large and formalized church-program. It is usually best, therefore, to try to help them participate in a smaller fellowship within a larger body. They may find warmth and friend-ship in a class for new Christians. A going Sunday School class may help satisfy their need for Christian fellowship. A small weekly fellowship of Christians meeting in homes may be a source of spiritual strength for them. By working with a small group, they can more easily relate to a larger one.

86

7. DEVELOP ANOTHER HARVESTER

The logical sequence which follows when our hearts are filled with Christ is our sharing the good news with others. A silent Christian is a contradiction. New people in Christ are often the most willing to share the good news. Given teaching and encouragement, they may soon take their place with other laborers in the harvest.

THE CARE-PROMISE IDEA

Many congregations today are familiar with the FAITH-PROMISE concept in missionary giving. A definite goal is established. Following a period of inspiration and instruction, members of the congregation are given an opportunity to commit a part of their income to global missions. Some churches have revolutionized their missionary giving through the FAITH-PROMISE idea.

The CARE-PROMISE idea works in a similar way. Members of the congregation are asked to commit their lives to the winning of others to Jesus Christ. Some congregations have been revolutionized in church growth through the CARE-PROMISE commitment. Following a period of teaching and motivation sometimes called "A School of Evangelism," Christians are asked to commit themselves to a definite goal in soul-winning. The emphasis throughout is upon the idea of every Christian an evangelist.

The card below is a sample. If this book is utilized in some kind of group study, it would naturally follow to close the class with a commitment service.

Cut out on dotted line.

"The harvest is plentiful, but the laborers are few;

CARE-PROMISE

Because I care, I promise to try with God's help to win _____ people to Christ during the next _____ months.

Name _____

Date _____

pray therefore the Lord of the harvest to send out laborers into his harvest." —Matt. 9:37, 38

FOOTNOTES AND REFERENCES

Chapter I

One of the best books written on the resurrection of Jesus Christ is by Frank Morison entitled *Who Moved the Stone?* My copy is on loan, at present, for a skeptical friend. C. S. Lewis in his book *Miracles* deals with the entire problem of the supernatural which is so difficult for many today who have been influenced by rationalistic thought.

The Spreading Flame by F. F. Bruce is a good place to begin in the study of the penetration of the gospel into the first century world. For a contrasting over-all view (with which I disagree) one should investigate Hans Conzelmann, *The Theology of St. Luke.*

Mandate to Witness by Leander Keck is a fine study of the growth of the gospel in a world without Christendom. Donald A. McGavran in his *How Churches Grow* has a section on the Bible and mission. One should also consult Roland Allen's *Missionary Methods: St. Paul's or Ours?* and *The Inescapable Calling* by R. K. Strachan.

Those with a critical background in New Testament studies are well aware that I have followed a traditional view of authorship. The Pauline authorship of Ephesians and the Pastorals is strongly disputed by some scholars. For a conservative study, one should read Donald Guthrie, *Introduction to the New Testament*. *Introduction to the New Testament* by Feine, Behm, and Kümmel will provide a more critical backdrop.

Chapter II & III

The Master Plan of Evangelism by Robert E. Coleman is a good introduction to the evangelistic methodology of Jesus. Where the word "witness" occurs in this study relating to contemporary Christian activity, I have tried to use it in the sense of "witness to something" as Timothy was instructed (cf. II Tim. 1:8). The Biblical idea of scattering in witness may be viewed in its practical application through the studies of Evangelism-in-Depth in Latin America. Included in these studies should be *Revolution in Evangelism* by W. Dayton Roberts and *Church Growth through Evangelism-in-Depth* by Malcom Bradshaw. An interpretation of the mission of the twelve and the seventy (in some manuscripts "seventy-two") may be gained by reading "The Mission of the Disciples and the Mission Charge: Matthew 10 and Parallels" in the *Journal of Biblical Literature*, Volume LXXXIX, March, 1970.

Douglas A. Dickey gave me the idea for the diagrams in chapter two.

In discussing the concept of the ministry of believers, start with *Salty Christians* by Hans-Ruedi Weber, move through *God's Frozen People* by Mark Gibbs and T. Ralph Morton and go on to *A Theology of the Laity* by Henrik Kraemer. Problems relating to the American minister are set forth in a study entitled "The Minister As a Preacher and Evangelist" (mimeographed) by Paul Benjamin. One should also read Elton Trueblood's *The Incendiary Fellowship*. Another fine study relating to the ministry of believers is Markus Barth's *The Broken Wall*.

Chapter IV

Contrasting points of view regarding revivalism and Christian education may be gained by reading *Religious Affections* by Jonathan Edwards and *Christian Nurture* by Horace Bushnell. The backdrop for obtaining a picture of the whole American church scene is available through William Warren Sweet's *The Story of Religion in America* and Winthrop Hudson's *Religion in America*. See also *A Religious History of America* by Edwin A. Gaustad. *Revivalism and Social Reform* by Timothy L. Smith lays to rest the ghost which says that evangelism and social concern are polar opposites. I am also indebted in this study of the Sunday School to Richard Myers of Indianapolis, although he must not be held responsible for my conclusions. *Teach or Perish!* by James DeForest Murch underlines the imperative for Christian teaching today. His older work, *Christian Education and the Local Church,* has interesting material on the Sunday School.

Chapter V

A study of urbanization and its impact upon the American church may be gained by reading Murray H. Lieffer's *The Effective City Church.* A strictly sociological viewpoint of urbanization is available in *Urban Society* by Noel P. Gist and Sylvia Gist Fava. No one has impressed upon me the importance of planting new congregations more than Donald A. McGavran. It is very distressing to me that this principle of church growth is being followed so distantly by many congregations today. Some Christian leaders may demur from my emphasis upon congregational initiative in establishing new churches.

Chapter VI

Perhaps no other chapter in this study is "mine" in the same sense as this one. The con-clusions to which I have come have been gained over years of conversation and through reading and experience. Many books touch upon "The Principle of the Kingdom of God Above the Institution" but none perhaps in this same way. At least, I have not seen them. *Struggle for Integrity* by Walter L. Knight comes close, and most of us are indebted to Keith Miller at this point. I am convinced that we must steer between the Scylla of being anti-institutional and the Charybdis of institutionalism.

Chapter VII

This chapter is probably the most important one of this study. Good theory and good practice must always remain twin sisters. *The Strategy of Evangelism* by Charles S. Mueller is a good practical study, along with an older but very solid work by George E. Sweazy entitled *Effective Evangelism*. Also valuable is the evangelism resource book *Reaching People for Christ* edited by Armand H. Ulbrich. The gap which must yet be bridged is the one between the concerned Christian and his actual participation in the work of evangelism. Here is the place where a career minister with the heart of an evangelist can work an in-service-training program with results which often seem astonishing.